Dark Water:
A collection of poems
By: Iona Henry

Edited by: Mario A. Thomas
Cover photo by: Juilan Hofer

Copyright © 2024 by Iona Henry

All rights reserved. No part of this publication may be reproduced, distributed or transmitted in any form or by any means, without prior written permission.

Dark Water / Iona Henry -- 1st ed.
1st printing August 2024
ISBN: 978-0-578-81688-3

~ Acknowledgements ~

Thank you to everyone who has had a positive impact on my journey.

Table of Contents

Part I:
Balance **01**
America's Paradise… 03
Casualties… 04
How Many?… 05
Micro… 06
Resiliency 07
How to Survive...08

Part II:
Peace **09**
Alone… 11
Cornerstone…..12
Pain… 13
Fear… 14
Inner Peace… 15
Transport… 16

Part III:
Everything **17**
Mother is Everything… 19
Child's Play… 20
Occupancy… 21
Her Eyes… 22
Within… 23
Existence…...24

Part I.

Balance

"Calamity has its roots in prosperity, prosperity has its roots in calamity."

- **Chinese Proverb**

America's Paradise

Too poor to tour the very land which is my own.

Too poor to afford the luxury to leave.

Being "Native" isn't all that it's cracked up to be.

Yes, I'm on island time and I can visit whichever beach I please.

But basically, that's all tourists see.

Don't you see the potholes,
the unpaved roads,
the poverty?

Do you see the government taking advantage ah we?

The unhinged citizens walking around aimlessly?

Have you seen the conditions of our schools,
Elementary and Secondary?

And try not to get sick while you're here,
you wouldn't want to visit Juan F. Luis.

I say this to remind you, this may be paradise to you,
but it's reality to me.

Casualties

Medical experiments
A man on the Moon
the government funds these,
but children on Earth will starve to death soon.

Concentration camps on US soil.
Genocide, homicide, the noose was tied
the moment we arrived.

Discrimination in housing, education, and medicine,
how can we survive, if we weren't meant to win?

The color of our skin is seen as a sin.
Christianity was used to teach us to speak, to think, to sing.

Negro spirituals were sung so we could cope,
but we've been coping since day one and never lost hope.

We're a casualty of European society and slavery,
where Indoctrination was the key.

How Many?

How many revolutions around the sun do we have to take before we get it right?

How many times do I have to watch the news and be traumatized?

How many of our people are going to die because "something didn't seem right?"

How many times is the revolution going to be televised?

How many protests will it take to save our lives?

How many times will hate crimes go unrecognized?

How many more questions do we need to ask, before you do things right?

Can you answer these questions, so we could move on with our lives?

Micro

Enslaved by microchips and microwaves

Micro aggression sweeping the nation like a tidal wave

Forced to be enclosed in boxes, even before the grave

Enslaved in our minds by the "American Dream"

But all we're faced with are American nightmares

Scream if you're terrified, laugh if you're scared

Trauma is the new drama

Watch and be amazed!

Resiliency (Independence)

You break me down
to build me up.

Sell me, buy me,
transfer, and brand me.

I am yours to offer,
and like sheep to a slaughter, I follow.

In the palm of your hand,
I lay me down,
I do not resist.

Still, I am resilient and one day I will be set free.

But, if I'm being honest,
being without you, somehow frightens me.

I've seen what independence can do.
I've seen it with Haiti and Jamaica too.

But with you,
I have rights, benefits, and if anything goes wrong,
you're always there to assist.

Still, I am an island of resiliency,
ready to break free.

How to Survive

You can't look back,
Don't seem suspicious.

You can't sell that,
You need their permission.

You can't drive that car,
Your tint is too dark.

You can't go too far,
You have too much ambition.

You can't speak to his daughter,
I can't speak to his son.

We must protect our black bodies.
Children of the sun,
For they burn too easily when it's all said and done.

Part II.

Peace

"He that knows patience, knows peace."

- Chinese Proverb

Alone

I exist,
but only in blood and bones.

I have been broken beyond repair.

I smile, to prevent more breakage, to prevent more stares.

I exist,
but only in blood and bones.

My bondage is flesh.
My prison is home.

I prepare myself for supper,
it is a meal I must eat alone.

I eat as a carnivore would;
Blood, flesh, and bones.

My battered body has been pulled apart,
broken.

I exist,
but only in blood and flesh.

Alone.

Cornerstone

You were the stone that the builder refused.

But you withstood the test of time.

A steppingstone for those who needed more
than empty promises.

You were the light.

You were chosen by God to rebuild the broken,
to restore what's right.

A safe haven for those who needed refuge.

A vessel of love and light.

And now that the broken have been rebuilt,
they must stand up
as you remain a vessel
and a pillar for what's right.

Pain

Pain latches itself to that hollow corner of your heart and spreads throughout your body.

Some call it anxiety, while others search for what they think it could be.

Pain can be a restless night,
A day of fatigue,
or even a life of strife.

But one thing pain cannot do,
is hide.

Pain is an illness,
something we can't disguise.

But make no mistake,
we all go through Pain.

So, we must choose him wisely.

Fear

Fear festers beneath the surface
his corpse is rotten and serves no purpose.

Fear lingers, his stench is pungent.

He cripples the hearts of even the bravest soldiers.

He feeds off his victims, rendering them helpless with useless emotions.

Fear of the unspoken, fear of the unknown, fear of being broken.

We fear the things we envision, things we do not know.
We even fear the things we want the most.

Once Fear has entered your life, he is hard to escape.
The only cure for Fear is peace and faith.

Inner Peace

In this temporary we stay connected
as the energy we manifested continues to grow.

Heaviness in my heart as I try to utter these words in prayer,
"We will grow; we will prosper."

The prayer is short, and the pain is temporary.

With each passing moment, I seek acceptance.
Acceptance of my present; acceptance of my fate.

I will continue to pray, as my angels guide me and as my heart
eases from its pain.

Transport

I run, I walk, I leap, I bleed.

I eat, I drink, I swallow, I feed
all in this shell that transports me.

Transporting my soul is this textured skin,
textured in blood, bones, and sin.

It has grown as I have grown.
Arms, legs, limbs;
each growing, as my soul remains the same.

The only constant I have ever known.

I run, I walk, I leap, I bleed
as this textured shell of blood and bones
continues to protect me.

Part III.

Everything

"Family is not an important thing. It's everything."

- Chinese Proverb

Mother is Everything

Our mothers are magical,
Full of life and passion.

Our mothers are spiritual,
Full of faith and compassion.

Our mothers are cynical,
Full of judgement and curiosity.

Our mothers are queens,
So, address them as "Your majesty."

Our mothers are multidimensional beings,
Full of everything.

My mother was my everything
May she rest in eternity.

Child's Play

Skipping over lies, lives, and lilies,
the children have no time to play.

Burdened by their parents' decisions,
secrets in dark, tight corners, come out to play.

Sins so secure and sacred
not even you can say their names.

Blisters on lips and knuckles,
you fight just to stay in their good grace.

Taking care of your parents' responsibilities,
you have no time to act your age.

You're aging faster than you expected,
still trying to keep secrets locked in your parents' cage.

The Children have no time to play.

Occupancy

You occupy space, room, time;
you occupy the corner of my eye.

The manic chambers from which you came
were too occupied to have feelings,
a heart.

Which is why you lay dormant,
you do nothing.

They threw everything but love at your wounds;
salt, shame, silence.

None of which can help you now.

You have wished many times to occupy their chambers,
but it has become vacant.

It is an airy room for a shoe, a glass or two.
It has become a showroom
to display everything, but you.

You occupy space, room, time;
you occupy the corner of my eye.

And as time passes, you become the very chambers
you once occupied.

Her Eyes

Behind her eyes, I see sorrow and pain;
she seeks neither, but both enter her life, unannounced.

Behind her eyes, I see power, mystery, compassion, and turmoil,
married with grandiose notions of freedom.

She'll never project these feelings to anyone,
especially to the ones she loves.

Behind her eyes, I see the compassion I thought had died with
the death of her laughter.

But like a Phoenix, she is reborn;
she laughs again.

Within

I find solitude within my skin;
this flesh protects my mind, my soul,
my sanity.

I find solace within me, myself, and I;
I find peace where chaos resides.

I find solitude within my skin;
my flesh, a supple armor
too tender to fight these earthly battles.

Within my flesh, my soul comforts me.
There is peace within me, myself, and I.

And as I seek more peace,
I close my eyes
and leave this world behind.

Existence

Time, the entanglement of memory and existence.

We exist in this Time of memory and clouds of illusion.

We are illusive to everything, even Time himself.

Through time, I have seen Time change, time and time again.

There is no time to change the past or think of the future.

The hands of Time will only stop, when our time has run thin.

Then and only then will our existence be written.

www.ingramcontent.com/pod-product-compliance
Lightning Source LLC
LaVergne TN
LVHW051923060526
838201LV00060B/4155